MOVING DAY

by

Karyn Finneron

original artwork by
Annemarie Provencher

Thank you for supporting a self-published author!

To order additional copies of Moving Day, contact:

Karyn Finneron
Massachusetts USA
kfinneron@yahoo.com

*Don't forget to mention how you would like the
author to personally autograph your book!*

*Book Designer/Editor: Julie Shissler
Original Artwork by: Annemarie Provencher*

*This book is dedicated to all the
grandmothers and grandfathers
who see their grandchildren move away.
It gives us all another place to visit,
but leaves tiny holes in our hearts.*

Annie woke up thinking about her Nana. She noticed that lately she seemed a little sad, and even short tempered. What was wrong? she wondered, usually Nana was so happy and just fun to be around.

She got up and went to the kitchen for breakfast. Her Mom, Dad and baby sister Emily were already sitting at the table. "Good morning, sweet pea," said her Mom. "Are you ready for some breakfast?"

Annie walked by Emily's high chair and made a silly face at her to make her laugh. As she sat down at the table, she gave a big sigh. "I guess so," she said.

"What's the big sigh for, Annie?" her Dad asked.

"Well, I was just thinking about Nana. She seems to be a little upset lately. Is she ok, Dad?"

Her Mom and Dad looked at each other and turned to Annie. "Well, Annie, you know that we are all moving to Nebraska soon, right?" her Mom asked.

"Sure," Annie replied with a smile. "We will be living closer to Grandma and Grandpa when we move. We'll get to see them more often than we do now."

"Yes, that's right," said her Dad. "I just think Nana is a little sad about us moving, because she knows she won't get to see you as often."

"Is Grampy sad, too?" Annie asked.

"Maybe a little," said her Dad; "but he is trying not to let Nana know that he is."

"Why, Dad? When I'm sad I'm not afraid to let anyone know," said Annie.

"Well, Annie, for grownups it can be different. Sometimes, they try hard to not show their feelings." her Dad said.

"Then, Dad, I don't want to grow up. I want to stay small and show people how I feel. I feel bad for Nana. What will she do when we move?" Annie asked sadly.

"Well," began Annie's Mom, "Nana and Grampy will come to visit us. You can talk on the phone and send them letters and e-mails and we'll come back to visit them too."

Annie thought about this. She couldn't help wondering what moving to Nebraska from Massachusetts would feel like. She knew that Nebraska was very far from where they lived now, because she had a big puzzle of the United States and her Dad had shown her where they lived. He showed her Nebraska, where her Mom grew up and all her family lived.

Annie had also been to Nebraska with her Mom and Dad, and she knew the plane trip took a very long

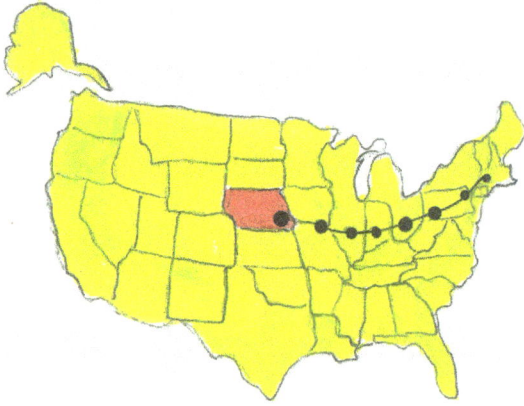

time. Nana had told her that she and Grampy had flown to Nebraska when Mom and Dad got married before she was born. At least she knew that they must know how to get to Nebraska. There was a lot to think about with all these moving plans going on!

"How will we get there this time, Dad?" Annie asked, for she had so many questions. "Are we flying? Remember when Emily went with me and Mom on the plane to see Nana and Grampy? It was hard for Emily to sit still for so long. Will it be like that again?"

"No, Annie. This time we will be driving, and it will take us longer than flying. It will be an adventure!" said her Dad. Annie smiled at her Dad but she was thinking about all of the things going on and she was not sure how this would all work. Mostly though, she was thinking about her Nana being sad about the move. What could she do to help Nana? She had to think of something.

"Dad, how many days before we go?" asked Annie.

"It will be about two weeks," her Dad replied. "Look, I'll circle the date we are leaving; here is today's date so we can check off each day as it gets closer." Annie watched as Dad circled the dates on the calendar, and then counted the dates from the first circle to the day when they would leave. It was exactly fourteen days to the big day!

"Dad, if we are driving, how long will it take? Where will we sleep? What about Emily's crib? What about our toys?' Annie was so full of questions!

"Slow down, Annie," her Dad answered. "Mom and I will take care of everything. It will be about two or three days to get there, we will sleep in a hotel, Emily will sleep in the pack and play bed. It will be fine. All of our things are going in the moving truck, even your toys."

"Ok Dad. So I have a little time to figure out how to help Nana not be so sad about the moving adventure, right?" Annie asked again.

"Right," said her Dad, "and you will be seeing her a lot before you leave, because she and Grampy will watch you and Emily while Mom and I do a lot of packing. Don't worry about Nana and Grampy. They would not want you to feel sad about moving," he added.

Hmm, thought Annie, they may be fine but how will we know, if grownups hide their feelings? I wish Emily was older, Annie thought; she could help me figure out what to do. Just thinking about all of this was making Annie sad.

The days started to fly by, and the dates were being checked off on the calendar. Soon Annie's house became filled with boxes and more boxes. Mom and Dad were always busy with packing clothes, dishes, toys; Annie never knew they had so much stuff! She helped out a little by watching Emily while Mom and Dad worked. Emily was walking now and she could always find something to get into. Sometimes she emptied boxes as soon as they were packed.

One afternoon, Dad said, "How about a visit to Nana and Grampy's house?"

"Yes," answered Annie, jumping up and down. "Can Emily go too?"

"Sure," Dad smiled, "I think your Mom and I need you two little monkeys out of the way, so we can get this packing job finished." Annie was excited. She loved Nana and Grampy's house, especially their big, fenced-in yard where she and her sister could run around. Even Emily couldn't find too much trouble to get into in that yard!

When they arrived at Nana and Grampy's house, Annie jumped out of her booster seat, while her Dad got Emily out of her car seat. "Go on, Annie, go ring the bell," Dad encouraged her. Annie loved ringing the bell. Usually Grampy would answer the door, saying in a grumpy voice, "Who's ringing my bell"? Annie would laugh, because her Grampy was never grumpy.

Nana was waiting for them with a smile; Grampy was ready to give Annie and Emily a big swing up in the air, asking "How are my girls?"

"We're fine, Grampy. We are here for you to watch us so Mom and Dad can finish packing," said Annie.

"I know, sweetie," said Nana. "What would you like to do today?"

"Hmm, let me think, Nana." said Annie; "We could work in your flower garden or make cookies."

"I'll let you decide," said Nana, starting toward the kitchen. "Pretty soon I won't have you to help in the garden, or to help me bake."

Annie thought her Nana looked a little sad when she talked about the garden and the cookies. She thought how Nana's cookies always made her happy, especially when they ate them when they were still warm. "Cookies!" shouted Annie. "Let's make cookies!"

"Good idea," said Nana, getting out the things they would need for cookies.

"How is Mom doing?" Annie's Dad asked Grampy.

"Oh, you know your mother, son. She will muddle over it; think of many ways to deal with it, and then she'll decide to accept the outcome. I told her, son, we have been so lucky to have all of our children and grandchildren so close to us. You need to live your own life. It will be fine," Grampy answered.

"Well," said Annie's Dad, "Annie has noticed her Nana is sad, and wants to make her feel happy again. She's a pretty sensitive little girl, Dad."

"Gee, son; I wonder where that might come from? She's a lot like her Nana, isn't she?" Grampy replied.

The afternoon flew by. Annie and Nana baked two batches of cookies, and Grampy took Emily for a walk in the stroller. When they came back, everyone snacked on cookies and milk.

While they were cleaning up after snack time, Annie looked up and gave her Nana a big smile and a hug. "I'll miss you Nana, when I move, but we can still talk to each other on the phone and on the internet," Annie said, seeing sadness in her grandmother's eyes. "Please don't be sad, Nana."

"I'm trying not to be, Annie," said Nana, "It is going to be a great adventure for you. You are so right. We will have lots of time to talk, and Grampy and I will visit. Don't worry." She smiled and hugged her granddaughter tight.

When Annie got home that afternoon she asked her Mom a question. "Mom, what do you think I can give Nana before we leave to help her remember me?"

"Annie, Nana is not going to forget you, just because you won't be living here," her Mom replied. "But it would be nice for you to give her something. What do you think she might like?"

"Well, Nana likes flowers, but they will just die and she'll have to throw them away. I want to give her something she can keep," Annie said, looking determined.

"I can tell by your face you have been giving this a lot of thought," said her Mom. "What if you and Emily give Nana some flowers to plant in her yard? Every year when they come up, she will think of you girls. Doesn't that sound special?"

"Mom, that is perfect! Can they be pink? Pink is one of my favorite colors," Annie smiled.

"Pink flowers it is," her Mom replied. "Tomorrow we will go and buy some pink lilies to plant in Nana's yard before we leave for Nebraska."

Annie was getting ready for bed that night, and telling Emily about buying Nana flowers for her garden – how every year when the pink lilies came up, Nana would think of them. "Isn't that a good idea, Emily?" Annie asked. Emily just smiled and clapped her hands; she couldn't talk yet.

"I guess she thinks it is a good idea, Annie," her Dad said. "Come on, you two; off to bed. Tomorrow

will be a busy day. You have to get flowers to plant in Nana's yard, and we have to load up the last of all of our things, so we can head off to Nebraska the next morning."

Annie jumped into bed, hugged and kissed her Mom and Dad, and tried to fall asleep. She was so excited about bringing Nana flowers. Flowers always made Nana smile. She was excited, too, about the trip to Nebraska. It would be an adventure, just like her Dad said. When they got there, even though she wouldn't see Nana and Grampy so often, she would have Grandma and Grandpa waiting for her. She was a lucky girl, she decided, and she fell asleep smiling.

The next morning Annie jumped out of bed and ran to the kitchen. It looked really different because all of the boxes and a lot of the furniture were gone. "Dad, where is everything?" Annie asked.

"Well, sleepy head, the moving truck is here and we are starting to load it," said Dad. Annie looked out the window. In front of their apartment house was a big truck with two men loading stuff.

"But Dad, if they take everything, where will we sleep tonight?"

"Don't worry, Annie. We have a blow up mattress and sleeping bag, and Emily has her pack and play to sleep in," he explained, smiling. "It will be like camping and we will get take-out for supper. The adventure starts today!"

"Wow, Dad, moving is a really big adventure," Annie responded. "I'd better go get dressed — we have to get Nana's flowers, go there for lunch and find time to plant them in the yard." She hurried to put on her favorite skirt and shirt and sneakers, brushed her hair and ran to the kitchen, saying, "I'm ready, let's go buy flowers!"

"Ok," said her Mom. "Dad and Emily can clean up breakfast, while you and I get those pink lilies for Nana's yard." Annie jumped into her booster seat in the back of the car; her Mom helped her buckle up, and off they went to a big nursery where there were lots of flowers.

There were roses, daisies, sunflowers and lilies too. Finally Annie found just what she wanted. "Mom, look at these. What kind are they?" Annie asked.

"Those are beautiful, Annie," answered her Mom. "They are called stargazer lilies, and Nana will love them. Look at the picture, they will be pink and white when the blooms open, and they will smell wonderful. Is that what you want?"

"Yes," said Annie, "two colors for two of us. That is perfect!" Annie was thrilled. Off they went to the cashier, and soon were on their way home with lilies for Nana's garden.

"Good," said Annie's Dad, when he saw the beautiful lilies. "Now we can go to Nana's for lunch and give her the flowers. She will be surprised and happy, Annie; it was a really good idea."

When they all arrived at Nana's house, she was sitting on her front porch, having a cup of tea. Annie got out of the car, and her Mom handed her the flower pot.

"Well, what have you got there?" Nana asked.

"Emily and I have lilies for your garden, Nana. We wanted to bring you something to remember us." Annie said.

"They are beautiful, Annie and Emily, thank you!" Nana said with a big smile. Annie thought to herself that she knew the lilies would be perfect and seeing Nana's smile made her know she had made Nana happy.

"Nana, can we plant them after lunch? Can I help you pick out a spot for them?" Annie asked.

"Of course you can, we will find a special spot." Nana said.

Lunch flew by and soon it was time to plant the lilies. Nana, Grampy, Annie, Emily, Mom and Dad were all in the back yard enjoying the day. "Well, Annie," asked Nana, "Where should we put these beautiful lilies?"

Annie looked all around and found a spot by Nana's back fence that had some sun and some shade. "How about here?" Annie asked.

"I think that's a great spot, Annie. It will brighten up that corner of the yard and make me smile every time I look at it," said Nana.

"Look, Nana. There are two blossoms on the lilies, one for me and one for Emily," Annie pointed out.

"Perfect!" said Nana. They dug the hole together and put the lilies in the ground. "See how great they look here, Annie." Nana smiled up at Annie. "Let's have your Dad take a picture of you, Emily and me, with the flowers."

"Can Grampy be in the picture too?" Annie asked.

"Of course he can, that will make it perfect," Nana said with a smile.

Annie, Emily, Nana and Grampy gathered around the freshly planted lilies. Grampy held Emily, and Annie had her arms around Nana. Annie's Dad took two pictures.

"They came out great!" said her Dad. "I will send one to your e-mail, Mom, and you can print it off." Nana and Grampy looked at the picture and both smiled.

"What a nice picture of all of us!" Nana said. "When the flowers open in a few days, I will have Grampy take a picture of them and we will send it to you." said Nana.

"Be sure you are in the picture too." said Annie. "I want to see you smiling when the flowers are open."

The rest of the day flew by, and soon it was time for Annie and her family to go. The day was full of laughter, memories, and of course the flowers that were planted. Annie thought it was a good day, but even she was feeling a little sad, now that it was time to leave.

"Well, Annie, let's pack up and go start our 'camping' adventure. We have to be on the road very early tomorrow to be off to Nebraska," said her Dad. "Give hugs and kisses to Nana and Grampy."

Annie ran to Grampy. "I need a big hug and a swing up in the air Grampy, I will miss the swings."

"I'll always have a swing ready when I see you, Annie. Don't worry," Grampy said. Annie got her swing, then Emily ran over to Grampy with her arms up, shouting "Me, Me!" That made everyone smile.

Annie went to Nana and gave her a big, long hug. "Thank you, Annie, for a wonderful day. Thank you for the beautiful lilies that will make me smile and think of you and Emily every time I look at them. Remember even though I won't see you as much as I did here, Grampy and I are always with you because you are in our heart forever." Nana was smiling and Annie felt good all over.

"Ok, off we go, everyone," Annie's Dad said. "Thanks, Mom and Dad, for making this whole day such a nice memory. As soon as we are settled in our own place, you and Dad have to come to Nebraska."

"We will son, have a safe trip, and keep us posted along the way," said Nana, with an extra hug.

Nana and Grampy stood on their front lawn, smiling and waving good bye. Annie thought how lucky she was to have them, and her Mom and Dad, and her sister Emily.

"I am a lucky girl," she thought, and she waved and smiled as the car drove away.

www.ingramcontent.com/pod-product-compliance
Lightning Source LLC
Chambersburg PA
CBHW070757050426
42452CB00010B/1874